EXPLORING SAND

AND THE DESERT

By Gayle Bittinger
Illustrations by Gary Mohrmann

Warren Publishing House, Inc.
Everett, Washington

Some of the activity ideas in this book were originally contributed by *Totline Newsletter* subscribers. We wish to acknowledge Pat Beck, Red Lion, PA; Denise Bedell, Westland, MI; Janice Bodenstedt, Jackson, MI; Reva Bucholtz, Tucson, AZ; Susan Burbridge, Beavercreek, OH; June Crow, Weaverville, NC; Marjorie Debowy, Stony Brook, NY; Sue Foster, Mukilteo, WA; Janet Helgaas, Luverne, MN; Ellen Javernick, Loveland, CO; Debra Lindahl, Libertyville, IL; Donna Malle, Fairhaven, NJ; Joleen Meier, Marietta, GA; Linda Moenck, Webster City, IA; Susan Peters, Upland, CA; Dawn Picolelli, Wilmington, DE; Barbara Robinson, Glendale, AZ; Betty Silkunas, Lansdale, PA; Judy Slenker, York, PA; Diane Thom, Maple Valley, WA; Kristine Wagoner, Puyallup, WA.

Editorial Staff:
    Editorial Manager: Kathleen Cubley
    Contributing Editors: Elizabeth McKinnon, Jean Warren
    Copy Editor: Brenda Mann Harrison
    Editorial Assistant: Erica West

Design and Production Staff:
    Art Manager: Jill Lustig
    Book Design/Layout: Sarah Ness
    Cover: Eric Stovall
    Production Manager: Jo Anna Brock

ISBN 0-911019-58-8

Library of Congress Catalog Number 92-62463
Printed in the United States of America
Published by: Warren Publishing House, Inc.
    P.O. Box 2250
    Everett, WA 98203

20 19 18 17 16 15 14 13 12 11 10 9 8 7 6 5 4 3 2

INTRODUCTION

Sand play is important for young children. As they manipulate sand they learn about basic math and science concepts, use language to describe what is happening and develop fine and gross motor skills.

Exploring Sand capitalizes on children's natural interest in sand and provides stepping stones to other opportunities for learning. After the beginning sand table activities chapter, there is a chapter filled with ideas for using sand around the curriculum. From sand in the art area to sand music, there are a variety of activities to help children explore sand in new ways.

Children learn more readily when they can move from the known to the unknown, and this book is arranged with that in mind. As your children become more familiar with sand, you can expand their interest into the desert. Place two or three plastic camels in the sand table. Tell your children that camels are found in the desert. As your children's curiosity is piqued, use the activities in the desert portion of the book to expand on it.

As with all Totline books, *Exploring Sand* is designed to be an easy-to-use reference tool, not a planned curriculum guide. You are encouraged to use whichever activities fit the needs and interests of your children. All of the activities in this book are appropriate for young children and use materials that are readily available.

With *Exploring Sand* as a resource, you and your children will enjoy the journey from sand to desert and back again.

CONTENTS

≋

Exploring Sand

Sand Table Fun

Learning With Sand

Exploring the Desert

In the Desert

Desert Animals

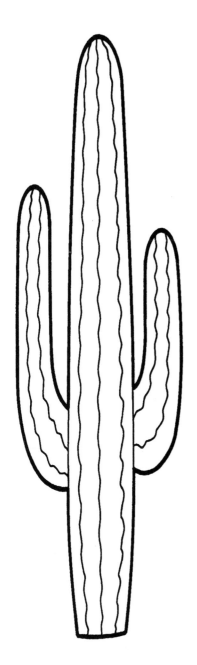

Desert Preservation

Desert Patterns

Children's Book List

Sand Table Fun

Basic Sand Table Props

Set out a variety of the items listed below for your children to use at the sand table.

- baking pans
- cardboard tubes
- craft sticks
- gelatin molds
- measuring cups
- plastic containers
- plastic tubing
- scoops
- spatulas
- spoons

Creative Sand Play Props

Fill a large container with props from the following list. Place the container next to the sand table and let your children choose items from the container as desired for creative sand play.

- birthday candles
- cookie cutters
- flags
- large buttons
- pine cones
- sea shells
- toy animals
- toy cars
- toy people
- walnut shells

Funnels

Cut plastic dishwashing liquid bottles or plastic bleach bottles in half. Show your children how to turn the top halves of the bottles upside down and use them as funnels in the sand table.

Hint: Save the bottoms of the bottles to use for building sand castles and sand towers.

Hanging Funnel

Screw four eye hooks into the ceiling above the sand table at the corner points of a square shape. Poke four evenly spaced holes around the rim of a large plastic funnel. Attach a thin rope to each hole. Tie each rope to one of the eye hooks. Adjust the ropes so that the tip of the funnel is 4 to 6 inches above the sand in the sand table. Let your children fill the funnel with sand and swing it around to make sand designs.

Hint: Let your children take turns making sand designs on a piece of colored poster-board.

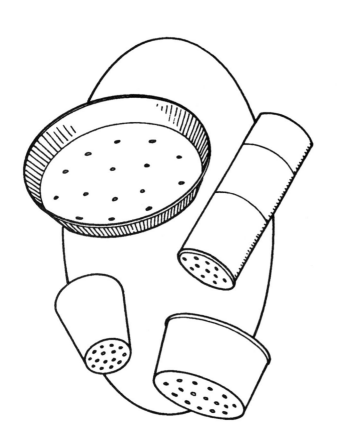

Sand Sieves

Make any of the following sieves for your children to use for sifting sand at the sand table.

Aluminum Pie Pans — Use a nail to poke holes in the bottom of aluminum pie pans. Smooth out any rough edges.

Plastic Containers — Use a nail to poke several holes in the bottoms of margarine tubs, yogurt cups or whipped topping containers. Vary the size and number of holes as desired.

Plastic Tennis-Ball Containers —Use a nail to punch holes in the bottoms or sides of empty, plastic tennis-ball containers.

Sand Pails

Collect several cardboard ice-cream buckets. On each bucket, poke two holes opposite each other near the top. Tie a piece of rope or thick yarn to the holes to make a handle. Cover the containers with colorful self-stick paper. Use the Sand Pails to hold props for the sand table. If desired, label each pail with the names of the items stored inside.

Sand Table Fun

Sand Combs

Cut rectangles out of heavy cardboard. On one side of each piece of cardboard, cut a set of notches. Vary the kinds of notches made on each piece. (See illustration.) Let your children use the cardboard rectangles to "comb" patterns in the sand.

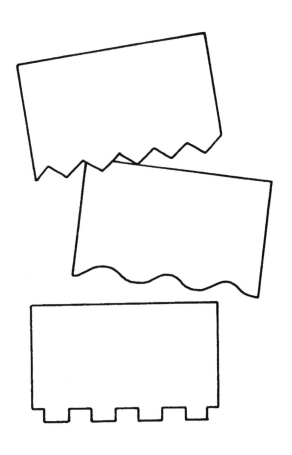

Spray Bottles

Fill several spray bottles with water. Let your children spray water on the sand as desired to make the sand damp and easy to mold.

Hint: To dry the sand, leave the cover off the sand table for a few days.

Sockdozer

Fill an old athletic sock with 1½ cups sand. Tie the top of the sock into a knot or tie a piece of twine around the top. Let the children drag the sock in the sand to make ditches and designs.

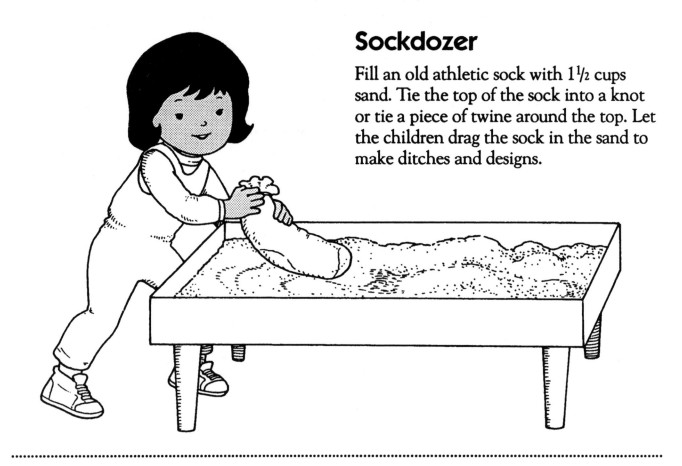

Measuring Can

Rinse and dry out an empty Parmesan-cheese container. Let your children use it to experiment with the concepts *more* and *less* by rotating the top for different pouring amounts.

Hiding Game

Ask two or three of your children to make mounds in the sand at the sand table. Then have the children close their eyes while you hide a small plastic toy in one of the mounds. Have the children open their eyes and search in the mounds of sand for the toy. Let the child who finds the toy first hide it the next time.

Funnel Race

Collect four funnels of various sizes. Give each funnel to a different child. Have the children hold the funnels over the sand table and pour sand through them for a specified time. Which funnel made the biggest mountain of sand? Compare the results with the sizes of the funnels.

Sand Table Fun

Sand Towers

Collect tin cans of all sizes. Smooth out any roughness around the edges of the cans. Show your children how to fill a can with damp sand, pat the sand until it is firm, turn the can upside down and slip it off to make a sand tower. Ask them to try to stack a small tower on top of a big tower. Can they stack a big tower on a small tower? How many towers can they stack on top of each other before they all fall down?

Sizing Up Sand

Collect plastic containers of various sizes to use as sand molds. Have your children arrange the molds by size. Then have them make a sand tower with each mold, lining them up from smallest to largest.

Sculpture by Hand

Show your children how to use their hands like funnels to make columns of sand. Let them experiment with creating all different kinds and sizes of columns. Then encourage them to put the columns together to make sculptures, castles or buildings.

Hint: Place a wooden board widthwise across the sand table to make a solid base for building sand castles.

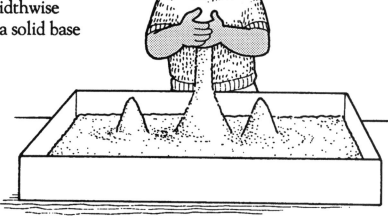

Working on the Railroad

Show your children how to draw railroad tracks in the sand with craft sticks or unsharpened pencils. Have them make the tracks go up hills, down valleys and around corners. Then give the children small toy trains to run over the tracks.

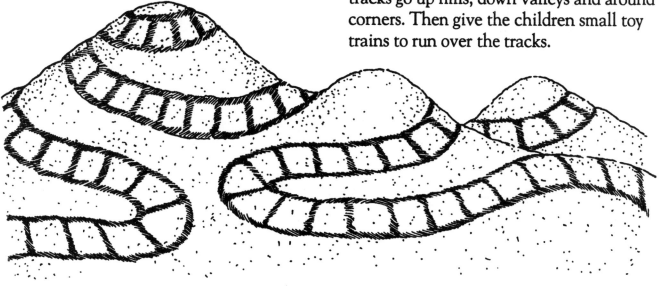

Feet-Only Digging

Make arrangements to move your sand table to floor level for a designated time. Make this time for feet-only digging. Have your children take off their shoes and socks. Then let them dig, design and build with their bare feet.

Sand Alternatives

Besides sand, let your children experiment and create with the following alternatives.

Dried Beans — Use one kind of dried bean or a mixture such as dried black beans and dried chick peas.

Macaroni — Dye elbow macaroni by adding a large amount of food coloring to a small amount of water and letting the macaroni soak until it is the desired shade. Allow the macaroni to dry.

Rainbow Rice — Mix food coloring with cold water and add uncooked white rice. Let the rice soak in the water until it is the desired color. Make several colors of rice, allow the grains to dry, and then mix them together for a rainbow effect.

Other Ideas — Replace sand with birdseed, cornmeal, crumbled cork, dry cereal, pasta, salt or aquarium gravel.

Individual Sand Tables

Prepare any of the following sand tables for your children to play in one at a time.

Cardboard Box — Cut down the sides of a sturdy cardboard box so that they are about 5 inches high. Fill the box half full with dry sand.

Dishpan — Pour several inches of wet sand or dry sand in an old dishpan.

Plastic Bathtub for Infants — Put wet sand or dry sand in an old plastic bathtub for infants.

Large Sand Tables

Set up any of the following sand tables for sand play by two or three children at a time.

Bathtub — Find an old bathtub that is no longer being used. Place it in a corner of the room and fill it with wet sand or dry sand.

Inflatable Wading Pool — Set up an inflatable wading pool and put several inches of wet sand or dry sand in the bottom of it.

Plastic Wading Pool — Recycle an old, plastic wading pool that can no longer hold water. Patch cracks or holes with duct tape. Fill the pool with wet sand or dry sand.

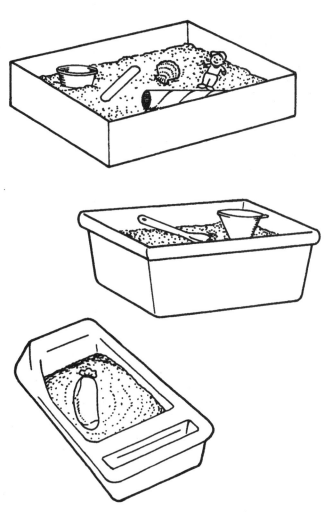

Learning With Sand

Sand Painting

Mix small amounts of sand with different colors of liquid tempera paint. Give each of your children a spoon and a piece of finger-paint paper or butcher paper. Put a spoonful of paint on each child's paper. Let the children push their paint around with the spoons. Add more paint as needed.

Sand Pictures

Let your children use glue to paint pictures or designs on pieces of construction paper. Then have them sprinkle pinches of sand over the glue. Let the glue dry a bit before having the children shake off the excess sand.

Sand Playdough

Mix together 2 cups flour, 1 cup salt, 1 cup water and a few drops vegetable oil. Add $1/2$ to $3/4$ cup sand until the dough is the desired texture. Let your children play with the sand dough. Encourage them to describe how the playdough feels as they work with it.

Permanent Sand Castle

Combine 6 cups sand with 1 cup Wheat Paste. (Recipe follows.) Add water until the mixture feels slightly sticky and packs firmly into shapes. Set out plastic containers for molds and a large wooden board or a piece of cardboard. Let your children work together to create a large sand castle. Allow the castle to dry overnight.

Variation: Give each of your children a small wooden board or a piece of cardboard for building an individual sand castle. Put all of the sand castles together to create a sand city.

Wheat Paste — Combine $1/3$ cup flour and 2 tablespoons sugar in a saucepan. Slowly pour in 1 cup water and mix well. Cook over low heat, stirring constantly, until thickened. Makes 1 cup.

Learning With Sand

Sand Jars

To make colored sand, place sand in jars with screw-on lids. Add the desired color and amount of liquid food coloring to each jar. Screw on the lids and shake the jars well to color the sand. Set out all the sand. Give each child a spoon and a baby food jar and lid. Have the children arrange layers of the colored sand in their jars to create designs. Be sure they fill their jars to the tops. Put a little glue around the rims of the jars and screw on the lids. Turn the jars over to display them. The jars can be used as decorations or paperweights.

Sand Castings

Fill cardboard boxes or plastic dishpans with damp sand. Have your children use fingers, craft sticks or unsharpened pencils to draw designs in the sand. (Be sure the children etch their designs deeply.) When the children are finished, pour wet plaster of Paris over the designs. Allow the plaster to dry. Write the children's names on the backs of their castings with a permanent marker. Carefully remove the castings from the sand to reveal the children's designs. Brush or rinse off excess sand and let the children paint their castings.

Variation: Instead of having the children draw designs, press each child's bare foot firmly in the sand (the imprint must be at least 1 inch deep), and then carefully lift it straight up. Then fill with plaster of Paris as described above.

Sandpaper Designs

Put glue into bowls and add a different color of food coloring to each one. Pour the glue into clean, empty squeeze bottles such as shampoo, hair coloring or liquid dishwashing detergent bottles. Set out sheets of sandpaper and the bottles of glue. Let your children squeeze glue on the sandpaper to make designs. When the glue is dry, have your children run their fingers over their designs to feel the difference between the rough sandpaper and the smooth glue.

Drawing on Sandpaper

Set out crayons and pieces of sandpaper and construction paper. Let your children use the crayons to draw on the sandpaper and construction paper. As they are drawing, ask them questions such as these: "Which paper is easier to draw on? Which paper makes the bumpiest lines? What happens if you put the construction paper over the sandpaper?"

Learning With Sand

What Is Sand?

Talk about sand with your children. What is sand? Where does it come from? How is it made? Set out sand, rocks, shells and magnifying glasses. Explain to the children that the ocean's powerful waves smash rocks and shells into tiny pieces, which we call sand. Then let the children use the magnifying glasses to explore the similarities and differences between the sand, rocks and shells.

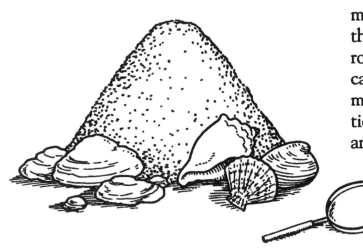

Making Sand

In sturdy, clear-plastic containers with screw-on lids (like the kind some brands of peanut butter come in) place 15 to 30 small shells, 4 to 8 small smooth rocks and $\frac{1}{2}$ to $\frac{3}{4}$ cup water. Screw the lid on tightly. Make as many of these jars as desired. Let your children shake the jars vigorously as often as they can over the next several days. Ask them to observe what is happening to the rocks and shells. Sand is beginning to form and can be seen on the bottoms of the containers when the water is settled.

Comparing Sand

Collect several different kinds of sand. Set out a container of each type and some magnifying glasses. Let your children look at the different sands. Ask them to make observations about each one. Then ask them to tell you how the sands are alike and how they are different.

Magnetic Sand

Collect some sand and let it dry completely. Put the sand in a flat, open container and set it out along with some magnets. Let your children run the magnets through the dry sand. Then have them examine the magnets for small black shavings of iron. Explain to the children that some sand is made from rocks that have iron in them. (Be sure to test your sand ahead of time to make sure it has iron shavings in it.)

Learning With Sand

Estimating

Set out a measuring cup, a box of sand and several different plastic containers of various shapes and sizes. Show your children one of the plastic containers and have them estimate how many cups of sand it will take to fill it up. Then add one cup of sand at a time to the container until it is full, having your children count out loud with you. Ask the children to compare their estimates with the actual number. Repeat with the remaining containers.

Predicting

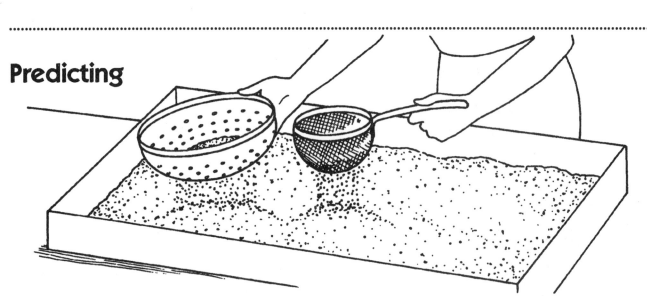

Collect three or four sieves that have various numbers and sizes of holes. (Or make your own sieves out of plastic containers.) Set out the sieves, a measuring cup and a box of sand. Show two of the sieves to your children. Ask them to predict which sieve the sand will go through the fastest. Then place the sieves in the box and use the measuring cup to fill each one with the same amount of sand. Pick up both sieves at the same time and let the children watch the sand flow through them. Which sieve did the sand go through the fastest? Was it the one they predicted? Repeat with a different pair of sieves.

Sandpaper Letters

Cut large letter shapes out of sandpaper. Glue the letters on heavy cardboard squares. Then let your children take turns tracing over the sandpaper letters with their fingers.

Variation: Instead of tracing over the letters with their fingers, let your children trace over the letters with pieces of chalk.

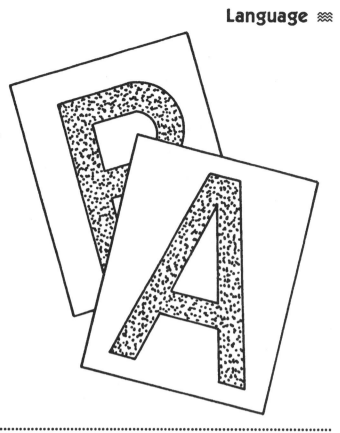

Writing in Sand

Place about 3 inches of wet sand in a dishpan. Show your children how to smooth out the surface of the sand with their hands. Then let them take turns drawing letters and shapes in the sand with a finger, a craft stick, a twig or a spoon.

Variation: On each of several index cards, draw a letter or a simple shape. Place one card at a time by the dishpan of sand and encourage your child to write that letter or shape in the sand.

Learning With Sand

In the Sand

Read the following poem to your children. Have them act out the movements as they are described.

I dig holes in the sand with my fingers.

    (Wiggle fingers.)

I dig holes in the sand with my toes.

    (Wiggle toes.)

Then I pour some water in the holes —

    (Pretend to pour water.)

I wonder where it goes.

    (Move hands out to sides, palms up.)

Elizabeth McKinnon

Sand Doll Family

Cut a rectangle out of heavy cotton or denim. Fold over one of the long edges about an inch and stitch to make a casing for a drawstring. Thread a piece of ribbon or a thin cord through the casing and knot the ends. Fold the rectangle in half, right sides facing. Stitch along the bottom and one side as indicated by the dotted lines in the illustration. Cut a slit as indicated by the solid line. Turn the bag right side out and glue or sew on fabric facial features. Fill the bag with sand and pull the drawstring tight. Make several dolls for your Sand Doll Family. Let your children play with the dolls. Encourage them to have conversations with the dolls and to have the dolls "talk" to one another.

Buried Treasure

Fill a box with sand and hide five small objects in it. Use small things such as shells, pebbles, pennies, beads or buttons. Let your children, one or two at a time, search for the "buried treasure." When they have found as many of the treasures as they can, ask them to count the objects or to match them to a card with a picture of each of the hidden objects on it. Provide a sifter for the children to use when searching for the treasure, if desired.

Mounds of Sand

Fill a dishpan with wet sand. Use your finger to draw a numeral from 1 to 5 in the sand. Ask one of your children to identify the numeral in the sand and then make that many holes in the sand in the dishpan. Repeat with other numerals.

Learning With Sand

Matching Shapes

Cut 6-inch squares out of heavy paper. Separate the squares into pairs. Lightly draw a different simple shape (circle, square, triangle, rectangle, star, etc.) on the cards of each pair. Carefully brush glue inside each shape and sprinkle on sand. Allow the glue to dry. Give the cards to your children and have them find the matching pairs. Ask them to name the shapes.

Variation: For a more difficult game, have your children close their eyes and find the matching pairs by touch.

Patterning

Fill a box with wet sand and smooth out the surface. Make a simple pattern in the sand using dots and short lines such as dot, dot, line; dot, dot, line; etc. Show the pattern to one of your children. Ask the child to repeat the pattern under yours. Do the activity again, letting the child make a pattern for you to repeat.

Variation: As your children become skilled at patterning, have them continue the pattern you make rather than just repeat it.

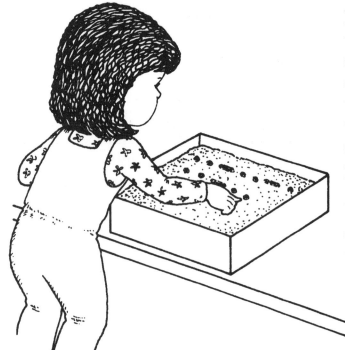

Learning With Sand

Wet and Dry

Collect two dishpans or boxes. Fill one with dry sand and the other with wet sand. On a tray, place wet and dry forms of the same objects such as sponges, sheets of newspaper, wash cloths and cotton balls. Let your children take turns selecting one of the objects and placing it on top of the matching wet or dry sand.

Sandy Textures

Set out six small boxes or tubs partially filled with dry sand. Add cornmeal to the sand in the first box, cornstarch to the second, oatmeal to the third, flour to the fourth and salt to the fifth. Add more sand to the sixth box and leave it as is. Let your children feel and explore the textures in the boxes.

Learning With Sand

Sand Pass Game

Have your children sit in a circle in a sandy area. Give each child a different sand toy. As you play some music, let the children play with their sand toys. When the music stops, have the children pass their toys to the right so that each child has a new toy to play with. Play the music again, having the children pass toys each time the music stops.

Follow the Trail

Use a stick to make a line in a sandy area. Have your children walk on the line. Try making a variety of lines: lines that curve, lines that have sharp corners, lines that stop and start, etc.

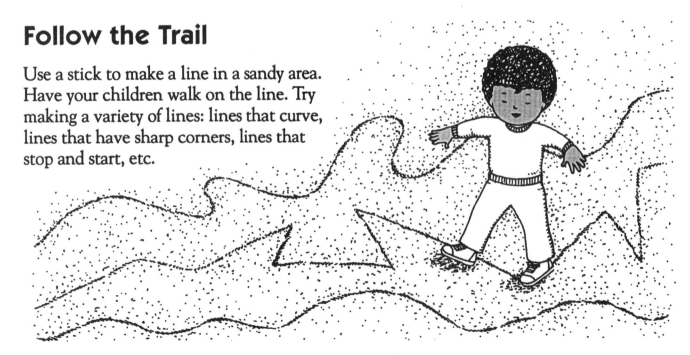

Learning With Sand

Sand Shakers

Give each of your children two paper cups to decorate with stickers and felt-tip markers. For each child, put a small amount of sand in one cup and place the other cup on top of it, rim-to-rim. Securely tape the cups together. Let the children shake their Sand Shakers while singing songs about sand.

Sandpaper Hands

Cut sandpaper into 1-inch strips. Wrap a strip of the sandpaper, rough side out, around each of your children's hands. Show the children how to hold the sandpaper pieces in place with their thumbs. Then have the children rub the sandpaper on the backs of their hands together to produce scratching sounds.

Learning With Sand

Sand Is Gritty

Sung to: "Frere Jacques"

Sand is gritty,
Sand is gritty.
I like sand,
I like sand.
Sand is many tiny rocks
Broken down from bigger rocks.
I like sand,
I like sand.

Susan Peters

Sandbox Song

Sung to: "Frere Jacques"

Make a sand cake,
Make a castle
In the sand,
In the sand.
Pouring, measuring, digging,
Pouring, measuring, digging,
Just feels grand,
Just feels grand.

Betty Silkunas

I Like Sand

Sung to: "Twinkle, Twinkle, Little Star"

Sand can be wet, sand can be dry,
I like both, I'll tell you why.
I make sand castles with wet sand,
And pouring dry sand feels just grand.
Sand can be wet, sand can be dry,
I like both, I'll tell you why.

Gayle Bittinger

In Your Hands

Sung to: "Skip to My Lou"

Mold, mold, mold the sand,
Mold, mold, mold the sand,
Mold, mold, mold the sand,
Mold it in your hands.

Pat, pat, pat the sand,
Pat, pat, pat the sand,
Pat, pat, pat the sand,
Pat it in your hands.

Sift, sift, sift the sand,
Sift, sift, sift the sand,
Sift, sift, sift the sand,
Sift it in your hands.

Continue with additional verses as desired.

Gayle Bittinger

Learning With Sand

In the Desert

Desert Facts

■ Deserts have extreme temperature ranges. Temperatures in some deserts drop from 126°F to 26°F within 24 hours.

■ Water is scarce in a desert. All deserts have less than 10 inches of rainfall each year. Rain usually comes in cloudbursts, causing flash floods. As soon as rain falls, the wind and heat evaporate much of the water.

■ Wind is a very strong force in the desert because there are no trees or mountains to slow it down or stop it.

■ Of all the land on earth, one-fifth of it is desert.

■ Only a small percentage of deserts are flat and covered with sand. Many have rocky mountains, others are covered with pebbles and plateaus.

■ Most deserts are found at the Tropic of Cancer and the Tropic of Capricorn latitudes, which are usually marked on a globe.

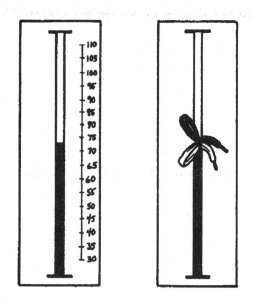

Hot and Cold

Explain to your children that deserts have hot temperatures during the day and cooler temperatures at night. Then explain that thermometers are instruments used to tell temperatures. To make a pretend thermometer, cut a small, narrow rectangle out of cardboard. Hold the rectangle with one of the short sides up, then make a horizontal slit near the top and the bottom. Mark the front of the rectangle with horizontal lines to resemble the degree markings of a thermometer. Cut a piece of white ribbon that is slightly more than twice as long as the rectangle. Color half of the ribbon red. Thread the ribbon through the slits and tie the ends together in the back of the thermometer. Show the children how to move the ribbon up and down to make the temperature reading change from hot (when more red ribbon shows) to cold (when less red ribbon shows).

Evaporation Experiment

Give each of your children a clear plastic cup with his or her name written on it. Mark each cup with a horizontal line. Then set out small pitchers of water. Have the children use the water pitchers to fill their cups up to the lines. Let them place their cups around the room. Have them observe the cups of water over the next several days. What is happening to the water levels? Why is the water lower than the lines? Explain to your children that the water is evaporating. Evaporation occurs when particles of water become warm enough to turn into a vapor and escape into the air. Did the water in their cups evaporate more quickly in warm places or cold places? Why does water evaporate so quickly in the desert?

The Desert Song

Sung to: "Three Blind Mice"

Hot and cold, hot and cold,
Winds that blow, winds that blow.
The desert is hot when the sun is bright,
It's cold when the sun goes down at night,
The wind blows everything out of sight,
In the desert.

Gayle Bittinger

In the Desert

Sand Dune Facts

■ In some deserts, the winds blow sand into piles, hills or ridges. These piles are called dunes.

■ Most sand dunes form when the wind blows sand against something sticking up from the desert's flat surface such as a boulder or a bush. Once some sand gets stuck there, then more sand piles up each time the wind blows.

■ Most sand dunes reach heights of 100 to 300 feet. Some are as high as 1000 feet.

■ The wind can move sand dunes as much as 50 to 100 feet in a year.

■ Sand dunes almost always occur in groups.

Making Sand Dunes

Let your children make sand dunes in the sand table or a large box. Have them make big dunes and small dunes. Talk with the children about how the wind forms sand dunes in a desert. Encourage them to make groups of dunes and to pretend to be the "wind" as they use their hands to move their dunes across the "desert."

Sand Dune Puzzle Game

Number five large index cards on their left-hand sides from 1 to 5. On the right-hand side of each index card, draw the appropriate number of sand dunes. Cover the cards with clear self-stick paper for durability, if desired. Cut each card into two puzzle pieces. Mix up the pieces. Give the pieces to your children and let them put the puzzles together.

The Wind Is Blowing Sand

Sung to: "The Farmer in the Dell"

The wind is blowing sand,
And piling it so grand.
The dune is growing very tall
From grains of sand so small.

Gayle Bittinger

In the Desert

Oasis Facts

■ An oasis is a small fertile or green area in a desert. An oasis occurs wherever water rises from deep within the earth or reaches the desert from hills or a higher source.

■ Oases in the desert are like fountains of life. Date palms commonly grow around them. Animals and people live near them.

■ An oasis is not permanent. It shifts locations or disappears when its water dries up or when it is invaded by a sand dune.

Oasis Art

Cut ovals out of aluminum foil or blue cellophane. Cut pictures of desert plants and animals out of magazines. Give each of your children a piece of tan or brown construction paper and one of the ovals. Have the children glue the ovals on their papers. Then let them select plant and animals pictures to glue around the ovals to create oasis scenes.

Oasis Hopping

Cut 15 or more oval "oases" out of blue construction paper. Tape the oases to the floor in a pathway across the "desert." Let the children take turns hopping from one oasis to the next.

The Oasis

Sung to: "The Muffin Man"

Let's go find an oasis,
An oasis, an oasis.
Let's go find an oasis
In the desert land.

There is water at the oasis,
The oasis, the oasis.
There is water at the oasis
In the desert land.

Date palms grow at the oasis,
The oasis, the oasis.
Date palms grow at the oasis
In the desert land.

Gayle Bittinger

In the Desert

Desert Nomad Facts

■ Desert nomads, such as members of the Bedouin tribes of the Middle East and Arabian peninsula, move about from place to place according to the food and water supply.

■ Many desert nomads herd camels, goats or sheep for their livelihood, and they rely on camels to travel across the land.

■ Desert nomads live in tents that can be easily put up and taken down. The tents can be lowered in height during a sandstorm so that they are less likely to be blown away.

■ The clothing desert nomads wear is designed to protect their bodies from the heat of the sun and blowing sand.

Desert Dress-Up

Set aside a corner for desert nomad play. Fill a box with clothing similar to what the desert nomads wear such as long robes, tunics, trousers that are full at the hips and tight at the ankles and sandals. A wrap for the head can be made by placing a rectangular piece of cloth over a child's head and fastening it in place with a piece of rope or ribbon. Be sure to include blankets for making tents over tables and chairs.

In the Desert

Who's Inside the Tent?

Have your children sit in a circle. Ask them to close their eyes. While their eyes are closed, quietly pick a child to sit in the middle of the circle underneath a blanket tent. Have the children open their eyes and try to guess who's inside the tent. Repeat until each child has had a turn being inside the tent.

Nomads Traveling

Sung to: "Twinkle, Twinkle, Little Star"

Nomads traveling 'cross the sand,
Traveling 'cross big desert lands.
Traveling through the night and day,
In one place they'll never stay.
Riding camels to and fro,
Watch the desert nomads go.

Gayle Bittinger

Date Palm Facts

■ The date palm was probably the first cultivated tree in history.

■ Date palms grow in northern Africa, the Middle East and around desert oases.

■ The stem of the date palm is straight and tall and is about the same thickness from bottom to top. The tree grows from 40 to 100 feet high.

■ A crown of large leaves grows on top. Each leaf is shaped like a feather.

■ The average date palm produces 100 to 200 pounds of dates per year. Dates grow in clusters on the tree and are red or golden in color. The dates can be eaten fresh or dried.

■ The date palm is used in a variety of ways. Its trunk provides fuel and building materials for fences. Its leaves are used to weave matting, baskets and bags. Rope is made from its fiber.

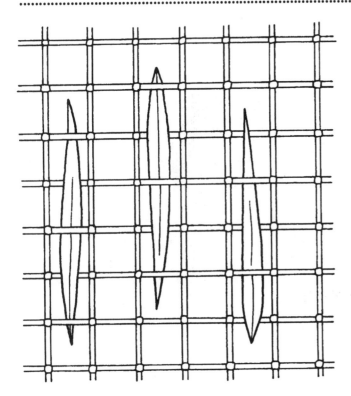

Weaving With Palm Leaves

Hang a lightweight fishing net between two chairs so that it is taut. Collect palm leaves. (Palm leaves are often available from a florist. If palm leaves are unavailable, substitute green ribbon or strips of green construction paper.) Let your children weave the leaves in and out of the holes in the fishing net to create designs.

In the Desert

Date Syrup

Combine 1 can (6 ounces) white grape-juice concentrate and 1 cup chopped dates in a small saucepan. Heat for 5 minutes or until dates are softened. Place juice and dates in a blender and puree until smooth. Return puree to saucepan and add $^3/_4$ cup water, $1^1/_2$ teaspoons cornstarch and $^1/_2$ teaspoon vanilla. Cook and stir until thickened. Serve as a dip for cut-up fruit or mix with plain yogurt for a sweet treat.

Dates to Eat

Sung to: "Frere Jacques"

Dates to eat, dates to eat,
Oh, so sweet, oh, so sweet.
Clusters grow near the sky
In palms that are so high.
Dates to eat, oh, so sweet.

Gayle Bittinger

Prickly Pear Cactus Facts

■ The prickly pear cactus looks like a bunch of spiny, flat, oval sections that are joined together. The cactus can grow up to 10 feet in diameter and 3 to 5 feet tall.

■ The prickly pear cactus is covered with spines. These spines deter animals from eating the plant, break up wind so there is less evaporation, and give the plant's surface a small amount of shade.

■ The prickly pear cactus blooms each year with red or yellow flowers. There are many different types of prickly pear cactus. The fruit of some varieties is edible and can be eaten raw or made into jelly.

■ The prickly pear cactus is found in the deserts of southwestern United States and northern Mexico, as well as some tropical areas.

■ The prickly pear cactus is becoming more common as desert grass is grazed away by cattle.

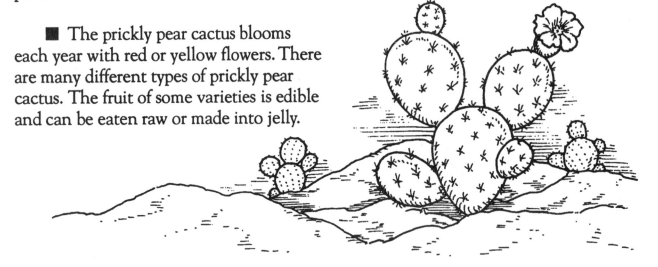

Counting Flowers

Use the prickly pear cactus and flower patterns on page 82 as guides for cutting five cactus shapes out of green felt and 15 flower shapes out of yellow or red felt. Number the cactus shapes from 1 to 5 and place them on a flannelboard. Have your children take turns identifying the numbers on the cactus shapes and placing the appropriate number of flowers on each cactus.

The Tale of the Old Cactus

Sung to: "On Top of Old Smokey"

Way out on the desert
That's covered with sand,
Lives a big old cactus
Who's really quite grand.

He lives all alone
Beside the old trail,
And if you just ask him,
He'll tell you this tale.

When he was a young boy,
He always played rough,
But he never was hurt,
For a cactus is tough.

But then one night
When he went to bed,
He felt a small bump
On the side of his head.

Now during the night
The little bump grew,
And the cactus got worried,
Oh, what should he do?

He called to the doctor,
And the doctor said,
"Don't worry, young lad,
It's all in your head!"

He called to his granddad
Who lived on the range,
"Don't worry," said Granddad,
"We all must change."

But he was still worried,
Oh, what could it be?
The bump on his head
Was so strange to see.

And then one day,
Before he knew,
Out of his bump
A flower grew!

Now the cactus is happy,
For this he does know –
We all must change
Before we can grow.

So if in the desert
A cactus you spy,
Wave to the cactus
As you're passing by.

Each cactus is growing
And changing each day,
And so are you
In your own special way!

Jean Warren

Adapted from *Carlos Discovers Change*
by Katherine I. Skiff

Flannelboard Fun

Use the patterns on page 82 as guides for
cutting a cactus shape out of green felt
and a flower shape out of red or yellow
felt. Place the cactus on a flannelboard.
As you sing the song to your children,
place the flower shape on the cactus.

Saguaro Cactus Facts

■ The saguaro (*suh-gwah´row* or *suh-wah´row*) cactus can grow up to 50 feet tall and weigh several tons. It is found in southern Arizona, southeastern California and northwestern Mexico.

■ The stem or trunk of the saguaro cactus is ribbed so that it can expand like an accordion when water is plentiful. The saguaro cactus collects water in its surface roots, which extend for many feet around the base of the cactus.

■ Many animals benefit from the saguaro. Hawks, owls and ravens nest in its branches. The saguaro has funnel-shaped flowers that bloom at night. When pollinated, the flowers produce a purplish-red fruit that is eaten by many desert creatures.

■ The spines on the saguaro cactus break up wind, deter predators and provide a little shade for the plant.

Saguaro Cactus Art

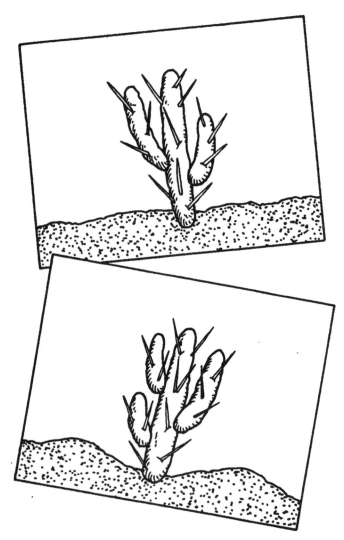

Give each of your children a piece of heavy paper. Let the children spread glue on the bottom halves of their papers and sprinkle on sand. Then give them green playdough and flat toothpicks broken in half. Have the children roll the playdough into fat "snakes" and arrange them on their papers in the shapes of saguaro cactus plants. Then have them stick the toothpicks into the playdough for spines.

Classifying Game

Collect several prickly items such as a cactus, a pine cone, a small broom with straw bristles and a hairbrush. Then collect several soft items such as a stuffed animal, a velvet ribbon, a piece of fake fur and a cotton ball. Draw a picture of a cactus on a large sheet of paper and print the word *prickly* underneath it. Draw a picture of a stuffed animal on another large sheet of paper and print the word *soft* underneath it. Put all of the prickly and soft items on a tray. Place the tray and the papers on the floor. Let each child pick an item and place it on the appropriate paper.

Did You Ever See a Cactus?

Sung to: "Did You Ever See a Lassie?"

Did you ever see a cactus,

A cactus, a cactus,

Did you ever see a cactus

Like the saguaro?

(Hold arms out like the branches of the saguaro.)

Saguaro, saguaro,

Saguaro, saguaro.

Did you ever see a cactus

Like the saguaro?

Additional Verses: Did you ever see a cactus that was so tall; that weighed a ton; with sides that expand?

Gayle Bittinger

Desert Animals

Ant Facts

■ Ants live and work with other ants in colonies. Each colony lives in a "nest." A nest is made up of rooms with tunnels connecting them. It can be found in many places, such as under a rock or in a mound on top of the ground.

■ A colony of ants includes worker ants (which are female), male ants and one or more queen ants. Most ants are worker ants.

■ Each ant has three pairs of legs. An ant's body consists of the head, thorax and abdomen. Ants use their antennae to taste, smell and feel. Most ants bite, some sting.

■ There are many different kinds of ants. Harvester ants live in warm, dry, sandy places. Honey pot ants live in the deserts of the United States.

■ Ants can be found in all the warm deserts of the world.

Giant Ant Hill

Cut a giant ant hill shape out of brown butcher paper and place it on the floor. Help your children draw rooms and tunnels all over the ant hill. Then set out several black ink pads and give each child a new unsharpened pencil. To make one ant, have each child press the eraser end of his or her pencil on the ink pad, then make three prints in a row on the ant hill shape. Let the children make as many ant prints as they like. Help them use black fine-tip markers to add six legs to each ant.

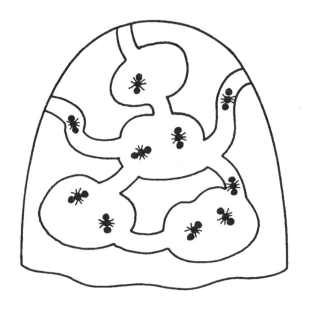

Ants in Nests

Number the bottoms of six paper baking cups from 1 to 6 and place them in a 6-cup muffin tin. Set out 21 raisins or small black buttons to use for ants. Let your children take turns placing the appropriate number of ants in each paper baking cup "nest."

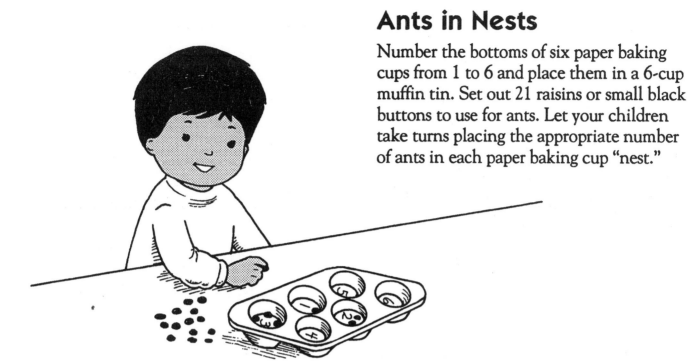

The Ants Are Busy

Sung to: "She'll Be Coming Round the Mountain"

Oh, the ants are busy, busy as can be,

Oh, the ants are busy, busy as can be.

See them dig and dig and dig,

Lots of tunnels, oh, so big.

Oh, the ants are busy, busy as can be.

Kristine Wagoner

Camel Facts

■ Camels can travel great distances across hot, dry deserts with little food or water.

■ The dromedary camel has one hump and lives in the Middle East, Africa and India. The Bactrian camel has two humps and lives in central Asia.

■ A camel can store up to 65 gallons of water in its body. The water is stored in the camel's body tissues, not its hump. The hump on a camel is a large lump of fat that can weigh 30 pounds or more.

■ Adult camels are 6 to 7 feet tall and weigh 1,000 to 1,600 pounds. Each eye of a camel has three eyelids to protect it from the sun and sand.

■ Camels feed on dates, grass, wheat and oats. They are ruminants, like cows, and chew their cud.

■ Camels are sometimes called the *ships of the desert* because some people get "seasick" riding on their backs.

Caravan Mural

Cut camel body shapes and camel hump shapes out of brown construction paper. (Use the camel patterns on pages 86 and 87 as guides, if desired.) Put a piece of butcher paper on a table. Have your children make a caravan of camels on the butcher paper by selecting camel shapes, gluing one or two humps on each camel, and then gluing the camels to the butcher paper. If desired, glue sand across the bottom of the paper to create the desert floor.

One and Two

Collect a variety of single objects such as a book, a comb, a toy car and a ball. Then collect a variety of object pairs such as two pencils, two shoes, two blocks and two cups. Mix all the objects together. Set out two boxes, one with a picture of a dromedary camel with one hump and one with a picture of a Bactrian camel with two humps. Let your children take turns sorting the objects into the boxes according to whether there is one or two of the same item.

Camel Song

Sung to: "Old MacDonald Had a Farm"

Here's an animal you should know,
C-A-M-E-L.
For carrying baggage, she's just swell,
C-A-M-E-L.
She's got two humps, or maybe one,
She lives in the desert in the hot, hot sun.
Here's an animal you should know,
C-A-M-E-L.

Debra Lindahl

Gila Monster Facts

■ The Gila (*heé luh*) monster is only one of two poisonous lizards known. (The other known poisonous lizard is the Mexican beaded lizard.) Its bite is usually not fatal to humans.

■ Gila monsters live primarily in southwestern United States and northern Mexico.

■ Gila monsters are about 18 inches long. They are brightly patterned with black and pink or brown and orange hues. The bright colors warn predators of the Gila monster's poisonous bite.

■ Gila monsters can live for months without eating because they store fat in their tails. They use the energy from the fat to survive. When they do eat, eggs and small animals are their primary diet.

■ Gila monsters are reptiles and, like all reptiles, are cold-blooded animals. They move around primarily at night and at other times when the weather is cool.

Gila Mosiacs

Cut pink and black construction paper into small squares. Set out the pink and black squares, white construction paper, glue and brushes. Have your children brush glue on pieces of the white paper. Then let them arrange the pink and black squares on the glue to make Gila Mosaics.

Cold-Blooded Animals

Talk with your children about animals that are cold-blooded. Reptiles and fish are examples of cold-blooded animals. Explain that these animals rely on the temperature of the air or water around them to determine their body temperature. Warm-blooded animals, such as dogs and cats, have ways inside their bodies to control their temperature. Then set out pictures of cold-blooded animals (lizard, snake, fish, shark, etc.) and warm-blooded animals (dog, cat, rabbit, cow, etc.). Show your children the pictures and let them tell you if the animals rely on outside or inside controls of their body temperature.

Gila Monster in the Sand
Sung to: "London Bridge"

Gila monster in the sand,
In the sand, in the sand.
Gila monster in the sand,
Don't you look grand?

When I see your pink and black,
Pink and black, pink and black.
When I see your pink and black,
I stand right back.

Gayle Bittinger

Desert Animals

Jack Rabbit Facts

■ Jack rabbits are found in North America, including the deserts of southwestern United States.

■ Jack rabbits stretch 2 feet from head to tail and are covered with brownish fur. Some have white tails and are known as white-tailed jack rabbits.

■ Jack rabbits have long ears, which help the animals stay comfortable in hot weather by cooling off the blood that circulates through them.

■ Because jack rabbits are born with fur and open eyes, they are considered to be hares. True rabbits are born without fur and with their eyes closed.

■ In the desert, jack rabbits get most of their water from the plants they eat.

■ Jack rabbits can run fast and rely on their speed to outrun their predators.

White and Brown

Use the jack rabbit pattern on page 90 as a guide for cutting two jack rabbit shapes out of brown construction paper. Add a white construction-paper tail to one of the rabbit shapes and a brown construction-paper tail to the other one. Put each shape on a separate box. Have your children search around the room to find white and brown things to put into the appropriate boxes. If necessary, set out some white and brown objects ahead of time.

Cooling Off

Do this experiment to show your children how jack rabbits use their ears to cool off. Put two hand towels in hot water. Take out the towels and squeeze the excess water out of them. Spread one towel on a table. Wad up the other towel in a ball and lay it next to the other one. Let your children feel the towels. Both of them are warm. Then let the towels sit for 1 to 2 minutes. Have the children come back and check the temperature of the towels now. Unfold the wadded-up towel. It is still warm. Now check the flat towel. It has cooled off. The more surface area exposed, the faster something cools off. A jack rabbit's ears are big so that the extra surface area can cool it off faster.

Have You Seen a Jack Rabbit?
Sung to: "The Muffin Man"

Have you seen a jack rabbit,
A jack rabbit, a jack rabbit?
Have you seen a jack rabbit
Hopping in the sun?

Yes, I've seen a jack rabbit,
A jack rabbit, a jack rabbit.
Yes, I've seen a jack rabbit,
A very fast one.

Gayle Bittinger

Desert Animals

Lizard Facts

■ Lizards are reptiles that are closely related to snakes.

■ There are 3000 kinds of lizards. All of them are cold-blooded and have scaly skin. Lizards move in a variety of ways. Some lizards swim, others walk on four or two legs, still others use their claws to climb trees.

■ Lizards range in length from a few inches to 9 or 10 feet long.

■ Lizards are the most common reptile found in the desert. When the sun is too hot, they lie in the shade or under the sand.

Puff Lizard Game

One desert lizard, the puff lizard, has a unique way of defending itself against predators. When the lizard is threatened, it will go into a crack in a rock or other narrow opening, turn around so it is facing out and puff up its cheeks. This prevents the puff lizard from being pulled out of its hole by its predator. To demonstrate this to your children, cut a hole just big enough for a child's hand to fit through in the side of a box. Put two balloons in the box, one inflated and one not. Have your children take turns trying to pull the balloons out the hole in the box. The inflated balloon is just like the puff lizard that cannot be pulled out of its hole.

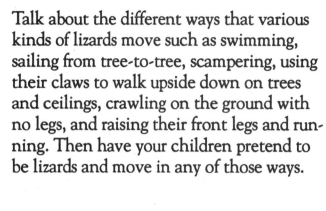

Lizard Moves

Talk about the different ways that various kinds of lizards move such as swimming, sailing from tree-to-tree, scampering, using their claws to walk upside down on trees and ceilings, crawling on the ground with no legs, and raising their front legs and running. Then have your children pretend to be lizards and move in any of those ways.

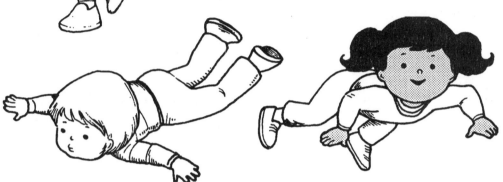

The Lizards Are Crawling
Sung to: "When Johnny Comes Marching Home"

The lizards are crawling everywhere,

Hurrah, hurrah.

The lizards are crawling everywhere,

Hurrah, hurrah.

They're crawling 'cross the desert floor,

They're crawling now and they'll crawl some more.

Oh, the lizards they are crawling everywhere.

Additional Verses: The lizards are sailing everywhere;
The lizards are running everywhere.

Gayle Bittinger

Ostrich Facts

■ The ostrich is the world's largest living bird. The average ostrich is 8 feet tall and weighs 345 pounds.

■ The ostrich lives on the plains and deserts of Africa.

■ The ostrich cannot fly, but it is known for its ability to run very fast, up to speeds of 40 miles per hour.

■ When an ostrich wants to hide, it sits down and stretches its head and neck out on the ground. It does not bury its head in the sand.

■ The ostrich drinks water when it is available, but it also gets water from the plants it eats.

■ Female ostriches lay their eggs in nests dug in the sand. The male ostriches sit on the eggs at night. During the day the males and females take turns sitting on the eggs. The eggs are 6 inches in diameter and weigh about 3 pounds each. A female ostrich will lay up to 10 eggs at a time.

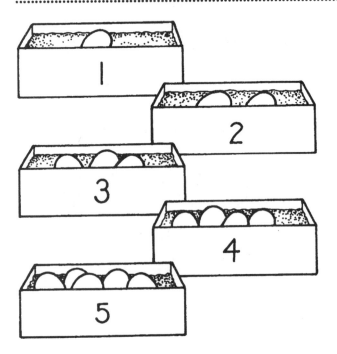

Eggs in Nests

Fill five shoe boxes with sand. Number the outside of the boxes from 1 to 5. Dig a shallow "ostrich nest" in each box. Set out the boxes and 15 plastic eggs. Let your children place the appropriate number of eggs in each nest.

Variation: Cover the numbers on the outsides of the boxes. Set out five different colors of plastic eggs. Let your children sort the eggs by color and put a different color in each nest.

Ostrich Kicks

Explain to your children that ostriches kick at predators with their strong legs. Take the children to a large open area. Have them pretend to be ostriches. Encourage them to run around and carefully kick with their powerful legs.

Funny Looking Birds

Sung to: "She'll Be Coming Round the Mountain"

Oh, ostriches are funny looking birds,
Oh, ostriches are funny looking birds.
They can't fly up in the sky,
But they run so quickly by.
Oh, ostriches are funny looking birds.

Oh, ostriches are funny looking birds,
Oh, ostriches are funny looking birds.
They eat plants and lizards for meals,
And if frightened kick their heels,
Oh, ostriches are funny looking birds.

Oh, ostriches are funny looking birds,
Oh, ostriches are funny looking birds.
Moms lay eggs in sandy nests,
Dads sit on the eggs and rest.
Oh, ostriches are funny looking birds.

Pat Beck

Desert Animals

Road Runner Facts

■ A road runner is a type of bird that lives in southwestern United States and northern Mexico.

■ Road runners earned their name because of the way they race down roads in front of cars, then dart off to the side. Other names for a road runner are chaparral cock, ground cuckoo and snake killer.

■ An adult road runner is about 2 feet long; about half of that length is its tail.

■ The road runner can fly short distances, but it prefers to run. It can run as fast as 15 miles per hour. While running, a road runner uses its tail as a rudder to help it turn and stop.

■ Road runners depend on the insects and snakes they eat to provide them with water.

■ Road runners make a *brrrt* sound when they are surprised.

■ Road runners build their nests out of sticks in low trees or bushes. The female lays from two to nine eggs at a time.

Road Runner Nests

Use the road runner pattern on page 90 as a guide for cutting road runner shapes out of brown construction paper. Cut egg shapes out of white construction paper. Set out the shapes, pieces of heavy paper, twigs and glue. Let your children glue the twigs on the paper in nest shapes. Encourage them to pretend that they are road runners making their nests. Then have each child glue one of the road runner shapes and two to nine of the egg shapes above his or her completed nest.

Fast and Slow

Cut out pictures of things that move fast (road runner, car, plane, horse, etc.) and pictures of things that move slowly (turtle, snail, caterpillar, tractor, etc.). Show the pictures to your children and talk about the difference between fast and slow. Then have the children stand up. When you show them a picture of something that moves fast, have them run in place as fast as they can. When you show them a picture of something that moves slowly, have them run in place as slowly as they can.

When I Race by You

Sung to: "Twinkle, Twinkle, Little Star"

When I race by, oh, so fast,
You will wonder what went past.
I can fly but I like to run,
All day long in the desert sun.
I use sticks to make my nest,
But I hardly ever rest.

Gayle Bittinger

Desert Animals

Snake Facts

■ Snakes are reptiles. They are cold-blooded and are covered with scales. The scales allow them to glide along the ground without friction.

■ Snakes live primarily in the tropics, where most deserts are located.

■ The tongues of snakes are forked. Because they have no limbs, snakes use their tongues for touching.

■ Snakes grow new skin several times a year. Shedding old skin and growing new skin is called molting.

■ Snakes cannot hear sounds carried in the air as humans do. Instead, they sense vibrations on the ground.

■ Snakes swallow their food whole because their teeth are sharp like needles and are not designed for chewing. They can go for more than a year without eating, but they usually eat more often than that.

Hunting for Vibrations

Have your children put their hands on a table. Hit the table several times with your hand. Explain to your children that what they feel are vibrations. Then have them hunt around the room for vibrations. (Loud music can make a table vibrate, a refrigerator vibrates when the motor is running, stomping can make the floor vibrate.) Can they make their own vibrations?

Desert Animals

Patterned Snakes

Cut 2-by-3-inch sections out of various colors of felt. Cut two snake head shapes and two snake tail shapes out of felt. Place the shapes by a flannelboard. Let your children take turns arranging the heads, sections and tails on the flannelboard to make brightly patterned snakes.

Variation: Place five or six felt sections on the flannelboard in a pattern and add the head and tail shapes. Have one of your children make a matching patterned snake below yours.

The Snake Goes Slither

Sung to: "The Wheels on the Bus"

The snake in the desert goes
Slither, slither, slither,
Slither, slither, slither,
Slither, slither, slither.
The snake in the desert goes
Slither, slither, slither.
Hiss, hiss, hiss.

Judy Slenker

Desert Animals

Spadefoot Toad Facts

■ Spadefoot toads are actually a kind of frog found in many deserts in Asia, North America and Africa.

■ Spadefoot toads use the spadelike growth on their hind feet to dig burrows. They stay in their burrows to keep moist.

■ Spadefoot toads mature from eggs to tiny adults in 12 days. The eggs are laid in temporary ponds that appear after it rains and must mature before the ponds evaporate. Other frogs take from several weeks to two years to complete the same process.

Sequencing Game

On index cards, draw simple pictures of rain falling, a pond, frog eggs, a tadpole and an adult spadefoot toad. (See illustration.) Show the cards to your children. Discuss with them how this desert frog develops after it rains, because that is when there is water for it to grow in. Then mix up the cards and let your children arrange them in sequence.

Burrowing Toads

Bury several plastic frogs or construction-paper frog shapes in a sand table or a box of sand. Have your children dig through the sand to find the "spadefoot toads." If desired, give them spades to use when digging for the toads.

Spadefoot Toad Song

Sung to: "If You're Happy and You Know It"

Oh, under the sand is where I'll be,
Oh, under the sand is where I'll be.
If you're looking for me,
You'll find me, 1-2-3.
Oh, under the sand is where I'll be.

Oh, I grow up so very, very fast,
Oh, I grow up so very, very fast.
When all the rain is past,
While the water still lasts.
Oh, I grow up so very, very fast.

Gayle Bittinger

Desert Animals

71

Desert Preservation

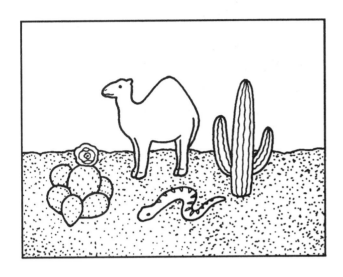

Desert Mural

Photocopy the desert patterns on pages 82–91. Make as many of each pattern as desired. Cut out the patterns. Place a long piece of blue butcher paper on the floor or a table. Have your children "paint" the bottom half of the paper with glue and then sprinkle on sand to make the desert floor. Shake off the excess sand. Allow the glue to dry. Hang the paper on a wall or a bulletin board at your children's eye level. Let the children attach the desert patterns to the paper any way they wish.

Hint: For more colorful patterns, photocopy them on colored paper.

Desert Landscape

Place a wooden board or a piece of heavy cardboard on a table. Set out bowls of green and tan playdough, along with other colors as desired. Let your children use the playdough to create a Desert Landscape.

Desert Preservation

Desert Colors

Collect orange, brown, tan, light green and yellow scraps of paper, yarn, fabric and ribbon. Show the scraps to your children and explain to them that the colors in the scraps are the colors of the desert. Then give each child a piece of construction paper. Let the children arrange the scraps on their papers to create colorful desert collages.

Colors of the Desert

Sung to: "Frere Jacques"

Desert colors, desert colors,

See them now, see them now.

Yellow, orange and brown,

Green and tan around.

Desert colors, desert colors.

Gayle Bittinger

Desert Preservation

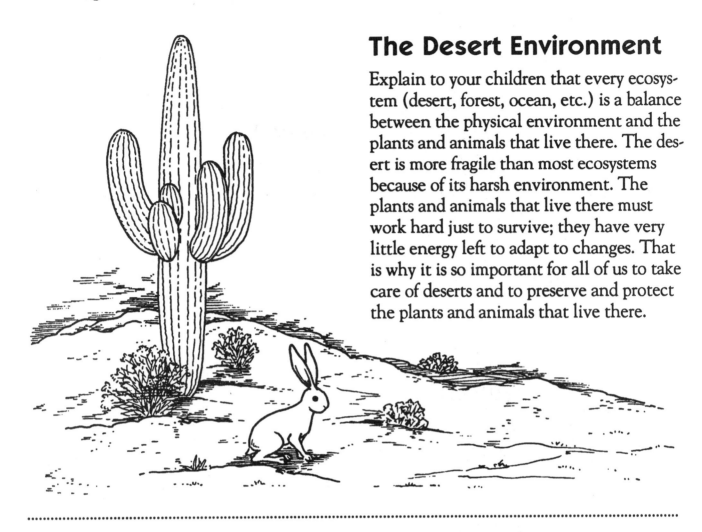

The Desert Environment

Explain to your children that every ecosystem (desert, forest, ocean, etc.) is a balance between the physical environment and the plants and animals that live there. The desert is more fragile than most ecosystems because of its harsh environment. The plants and animals that live there must work hard just to survive; they have very little energy left to adapt to changes. That is why it is so important for all of us to take care of deserts and to preserve and protect the plants and animals that live there.

Growing Cacti

Purchase two or three different types of cactus. (Prickly pear are fast growing.) Let your children take turns caring for the cacti. Have them measure the growth of each cactus on a chart. If desired, take photographs of the cacti as they grow. Let the children arrange the photos in order and dictate stories about them.

Desert Preservation

Web of Life

Photocopy the patterns on pages 82–91. Cut out the patterns and give each of your children one to tape to his or her shirt. Have the children pretend to be the plants and animals shown on their shirts. Ask the children to stand in a circle. Give a large ball of yarn to one child. Have that child hold the yarn and toss the ball to another child. Repeat until each child is holding a section of the yarn and the web is complete. Explain to the children that the web represents the web of life in the desert. Each plant or animal is connected to all of the others in some way. Then one at a time, have the children pretend their plants or animals have disappeared from the desert and let go of the yarn. What happens to the web after one child lets go? After three children let go? After five? The web starts falling apart. When each part of the desert is taken care of, the web of life can stay together just as the yarn web did when all of the children were holding onto it.

You Can Surely See
Sung to: "The Farmer in the Dell"

All of the plants,

And the animals too,

Are connected together

Like me and you.

The web of life,

Goes from you to me,

And to the plants and animals

As you can surely see.

Gayle Bittinger

Desert Preservation

Look and Gently Touch

Explain to your children that whenever they walk through a desert, they must remember the rule, "Leave it where you find it." Picking flowers or digging up cacti hurts the desert's web of life. Many desert flowers bloom and then turn to seed. These seeds lie dormant in the ground until the following year when they will grow into plants that will produce next year's flowers. If the flowers are removed, there won't be any seeds for next year. Take your children on a walk outside to practice this rule. Encourage them to look at and gently touch the things they find outside and to leave them were they are.

In the Great Big Desert
Sung to: "I'm a Little White Duck"

In the great big desert,

Where the sun does shine.

There are lots of plants,

But none of them are mine.

I look at them with my eyes so bright,

And when I'm done I leave them alright.

In the great big desert,

Where the sun does shine,

I leave them.

Gayle Bittinger

Desert Preservation

78

Desert Rules

Explain to your children that exploring the desert is fun. But there are also special rules to follow to stay safe and healthy. Share your desert rules with the children. Your rules might include some of the following.

- Always go with someone else and stay together.
- Carry water and drink lots of it.
- Keep hands and feet in sight.
- Stay close to the car.
- Carry a whistle and use it to signal for help when needed.

Draw simple pictures of these and other desert safety rules on index cards. Put the cards in a pile. Have two or three children at a time select a card and act out the safety rule for the other children to guess.

When You Walk in Deserts

Sung to: "The More We Get Together"

When you walk in deserts,
In deserts, in deserts.
When you walk in deserts
You must follow rules.
You must stay together,
You must carry water.
When you walk in deserts
You must follow rules.

When you walk in deserts,
In deserts, in deserts.
When you walk in deserts
You must follow rules.
You must see your hands,
You must see your feet.
When you walk in deserts
You must follow rules.

When you walk in deserts,
In deserts, in deserts.
When you walk in deserts
You must follow rules.
You must carry a whistle,
You must stay by your car.
When you walk in deserts
You must follow rules.

Gayle Bittinger

Desert Patterns

Prickly Pear Cactus and Flower

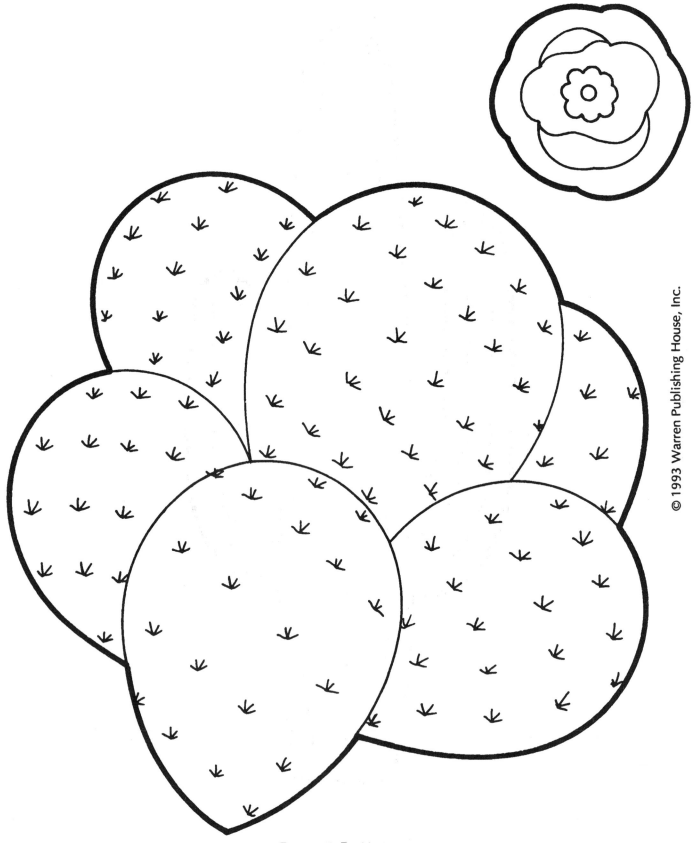

Desert Patterns

Saguaro Cactus

Desert Patterns

Date Palm

Desert Patterns

Ant

Spadefoot Toad

Dromedary Camel

Desert Patterns

Bactrian Camel

Desert Patterns

Gila Monster

Lizard

Snake

Jack Rabbit

Road Runner

Desert Patterns

Ostrich

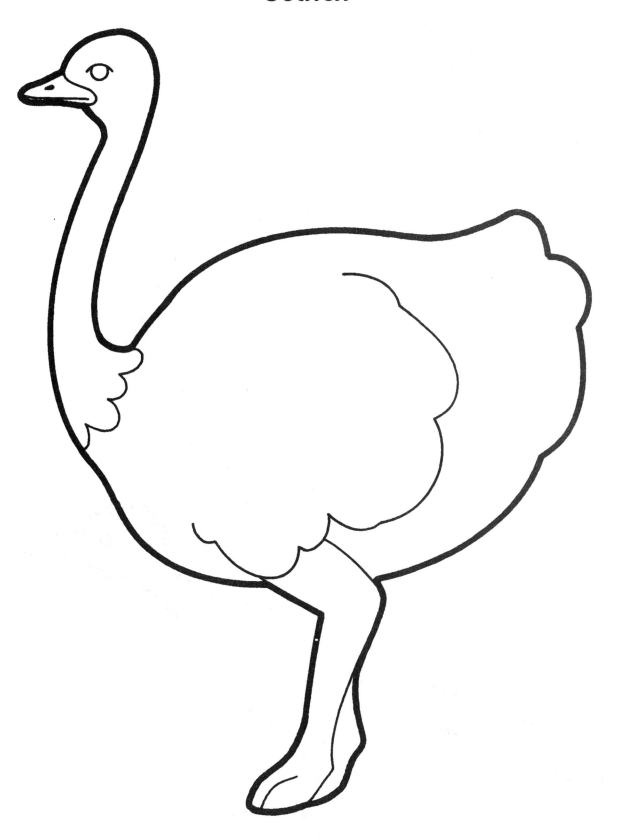

Desert Patterns

CHILDREN'S BOOKS ABOUT SAND AND THE DESERT

FICTION

Camel Who Took a Walk, Jack Tworkov, (Dutton, 1989).

Effie, Beverley Allinson, (Scholastic, 1991).

Gila Monsters Meet You at the Airport, Marjorie Sharmat, (Macmillan, 1980).

Hide and Snake, Keith Baker, (Harcourt, 1991).

How the Camel Got His Hump, Rudyard Kipling, (Picture Book Studio, 1989).

Johnny Castleseed, Edward Ormondroyd, (Houghton Mifflin, 1985).

Mouse Count, Ellen Stoll Walsh, (Harcourt, 1991).

Sand Cake, Frank Asch, (Putnam, 1978).

NON-FICTION

Ant Cities, Arthur Dorros, (Harper, 1987).

Cactus Hotel, Brenda Guiberson,
    (Henry Holt, 1991).

Desert Giant: The World of the Saguaro Cactus,
    Barbara Bash, (Little Brown, 1989).

The Desert Is Theirs, Byrd Baylor, (Scribner's, 1975).

Frogs, Toad, Lizards, and Salamanders,
    Nancy Winslow Parker, (Morrow, 1990).

Lizard in the Sun, Joanne Ryder, (Morrow, 1990).

Nature's Footprints in the Desert, Q.L. Pearce,
    (Silver Press, 1990).

The New True Book of Deserts, Elsa Posell,
    (Childrens Press, 1982).

A Night and Day in the Desert,
    Jennifer Owings Dewey, (Little Brown, 1991).

Snakes Are Hunters, Patricia Lauber, (Harper, 1988).

The Sun, the Wind and the Rain,
    Lisa Westberg Peters, (Henry Holt, 1988).

A Walk in the Desert, Caroline Arnold,
    (Silver Burdett, 1991).

What Is a Desert?, Chris Arvetis, (Macmillan, 1987).

Totline® Newsletter

Activities, songs and new ideas to use right now are waiting for you in every issue!

Each issue puts the fun into teaching with 32 pages of challenging and creative activities for young children. Included are open-ended art activities, learning games, music, language and science activities plus 8 reproducible pattern pages.

Published bi-monthly.

Sample issue - $2.00

Super Snack News

Nutritious snack ideas, related songs, rhymes and activities

- Teach young children health and nutrition through fun and creative activities.

- Use as a handout to involve parents in their children's education.

- Promote quality child care in the community with these handouts.

- Includes nutritious sugarless snacks, health tidbits, and developmentally appropriate activities.

- Includes CACFP information for most snacks.

Sample issue - $2.00

With each subscription you are given the right to:

Make up to:
200 COPIES
per issue

Warren Publishing House, Inc. • P.O. Box 2250, Dept. Z • Everett, WA **98203**

Hands-on, creative teaching ideas from Totline® books

PIGGYBACK® SONG SERIES

Piggyback Songs

More Piggyback Songs

Piggyback Songs for Infants and Toddlers

Piggyback Songs in Praise of God

Piggyback Songs in Praise of Jesus

Holiday Piggyback Songs

Animal Piggyback Songs

Piggyback Songs for School

Piggyback Songs to Sign

1•2•3 SERIES

1•2•3 Art

1•2•3 Games

1•2•3 Colors

1•2•3 Puppets

1•2•3 Murals

1•2•3 Books

1•2•3 Reading & Writing

1•2•3 Rhymes, Stories & Songs

1•2•3 Math

1•2•3 Science

ABC SERIES

ABC Space

ABC Farm

ABC Zoo

ABC Circus

CELEBRATION SERIES

Small World Celebrations

Special Day Celebrations

Yankee Doodle Birthday Celebrations

Great Big Holiday Celebrations

CUT & TELL SERIES

Scissor Stories for Fall

Scissor Stories for Winter

Scissor Stories for Spring

TEACHING TALE SERIES

Teeny-Tiny Folktales

Short-Short Stories

Mini-Mini Musicals

THEME-A-SAURUS® SERIES

Theme-A-Saurus

Theme-A-Saurus II

Toddler Theme-A-Saurus

Alphabet Theme-A-Saurus

Nursery Rhyme Theme-A-Saurus

Storytime Theme-A-Saurus

TAKE-HOME SERIES

Alphabet & Number Rhymes

Color, Shape & Season Rhymes

Object Rhymes

Animal Rhymes

LEARNING & CARING ABOUT

Our World

Our Selves

Our Town

MIX & MATCH PATTERNS

Animal Patterns

Everyday Patterns

Holiday Patterns

Nature Patterns

EXPLORING SERIES

Exploring Sand

Exploring Water

Exploring Wood

1001 SERIES

1001 Teaching Props

1001 Teaching Tips

OTHER

Super Snacks

Celebrating Childhood

Home Activity Booklet

23 Hands-On Workshops

Cooperation Booklet

Warren Publishing House, Inc.

Totline books are available at school-supply stores and parent-teacher stores.